WELCOME TO
MOUNT RAINIER
NATIONAL PARK

BY PAMELA DELL

Many thanks to the staff at Mount Rainier National Park for their assistance with this book.

MAP KEY
The maps throughout this
book use the following icons:

 Campground

 Driving Excursion

 Hiking Trail

Lodging

Marmot Viewing Area

Overlook

Point of Interest

 Ranger Station

Visitor Center

Wildflower Area

Wooded Area

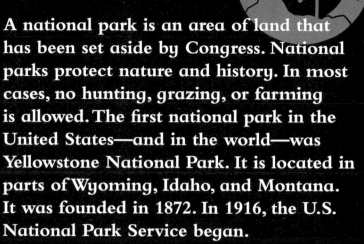

About National Parks

A national park is an area of land that has been set aside by Congress. National parks protect nature and history. In most cases, no hunting, grazing, or farming is allowed. The first national park in the United States—and in the world—was Yellowstone National Park. It is located in parts of Wyoming, Idaho, and Montana. It was founded in 1872. In 1916, the U.S. National Park Service began.

Today, the National Park Service manages more than 380 sites. Some of these sites are historic, such as the Statue of Liberty or Martin Luther King, Jr. National Historic Site. Other park areas preserve wild land. The National Park Service manages 40% of the nation's wilderness areas, including national parks. Each year, millions of people from around the world visit these national parks. Visitors may camp, go canoeing, or go for a hike. Or, they may simply sit and enjoy the scenery, wildlife, and the quiet of the land.

TABLE OF

The Child's World®

**Published in the
United States of America
by The Child's World®**

PO Box 326
Chanhassen, MN 55317-0326
800-599-READ
www.childsworld.com

Acknowledgements

The Child's World®: Mary Berendes, Publishing Director

Content Consultant: Michael Larson, Visual Information Specialist, Mount Rainier National Park

The Design Lab: Kathleen Petelinsek, Design and Page Production

Map Hero, Inc.: Matt Kania, Cartographer

Red Line Editorial: Bob Temple, Editorial Direction

Photo Credits

Cover and this page: Corbis

Interior: Alex L Fradkin/Getty: 6–7; Altrendo Nature/Getty: 10–11; Art Wolfe/Getty: 8; Bohemian Nomad Picturemakers/Corbis: 15; Charles Mauzy/Corbis: 1, 18, 21, 25, 27; Corbis: 14; Craig Tuttle/Corbis: 2–3; David Muench/Corbis: 12–13; Michael T. Sedam/Corbis: 17;

Library of Congress Cataloging-in-Publication Data

Dell, Pamela.
  Welcome to Mount Rainier National Park / by Pamela Dell.
    p. cm. — (Visitor guides)
  Includes index.
  ISBN 1-59296-700-0 (library bound : alk. paper)
  1. Mount Rainier National Park (Wash.)—Juvenile literature. I. Title. II. Series.
  F897.R2D45 2006
  979.7'782—dc22   2005030072

On the cover and this page
Some of the best views of Mount Rainier are from the air. Here you can see another famous Washington mountain, Mount Adams, off in the distance.

On page 1
The peak of Mount Rainier seems to glow with orange light as the sun sets.

On pages 2–3
Wildflowers such as lupine, paintbrush, and bistort cover many of the park's sunny meadows.

WELCOME TO MOUNT RAINIER NATIONAL PARK

CONTENTS

Nature in Balance, 6

Rain Gear Required, 10

Mountain of Fire, 12

Longmire and Paradise, 16

Ancient Trees, Giant Glaciers, 20

Far From the Beaten Track, 22

A World of Wonders, 26

Map, 28

Mount Rainier National Park Fast Facts, 29

Glossary, 30

To Find Out More, 31

Index, 32

Nature in Balance

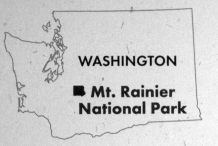

WASHINGTON

■ **Mt. Rainier National Park**

Welcome to Mount Rainier National Park! Have you ever wanted to explore a rare rainforest? What about a stroll through a wildflower meadow full of color? Would you like to stand beneath an icy blue **glacier** or gaze up at large trees that are 1,000 years old? This is the place to do all these things. Mount Rainier is located southeast of Seattle, Washington. It has a variety of plants, animals, and scenery.

From the top of Mount Rainier to the bottom, a dramatic change in elevation occurs. This makes each part of the park so **diverse**. Some plants and animals live only in one region. You will see others like deer, squirrels, and twittering gray jays in many different areas. Black bears, cougars, elk, and bats live here, too.

Elk grow to be about 5 feet (1.5 m) tall at the shoulder and weigh 700 pounds (318 kg). Like other members of the deer animal family, elk eat plants and are most active at sunrise and sunset. Elk are sometimes called *wapiti*, which is a Shawnee word meaning "white rump."

Marmot Crossing

Mount Rainier's most visible critter is probably the marmot. Members of the squirrel family, marmots are not shy. You might even manage to get quite close to one. Most often you'll find them munching wildflowers or dozing in the sun on a big rock.

All the plants and animals living together in each area depend upon each other to stay alive. If a plant **species** dies, the animals that eat it may die, too. Living things also need the climate conditions of their own region. This system is called an **ecosystem**. To survive, an ecosystem must keep its delicate balance.

By the early 1890s, thousands of people were coming to enjoy this wilderness. Local communities, scientists, and **conservation** organizations wanted to protect this ecosystem. Their efforts made Mount Rainier the country's fifth national park, in 1899.

This photo from 1910 shows visitors enjoying the park. You can see one of the men is even taking pictures! The park has been a favorite spot for photographers for more than 100 years.

Rain Gear Required

You can see the wonders of Mount Rainier in any season. The nearby Pacific Ocean keeps it cool—and plenty wet! Summers are short and mild. The fog rolls in early in the morning. It may burn off to clear blue skies. But cloudy days are common. If you are here for very long, expect to get drenched often by rainstorms.

Winter comes early and stays long. Storms with huge snowfalls come often. Some areas become impossible to reach. They may be closed for the whole season. The higher you go up the slopes, the colder it gets. This is true all year long.

Storm clouds often roll over the park's forests. Some areas get 100 inches (254 cm) of rain and 680 inches (17 m) of snow a year! Mount Rainier itself gets a little more rain and snow than other areas of the park—about 140 inches (356 cm) a year.

Mountain of Fire

You can't miss Mount Rainier. You'll see it long before you even enter the park. At an elevation of 14,410 feet (4,392 m), it is the fifth-largest peak in the continental United States. On a clear day, Mount Rainier can be clearly seen from more than 100 miles (161 km) away. One of its Native American names is "Tahoma," which is thought to mean, "Big Mountain." No wonder!

If you choose to climb to the top of Mount Rainier, be prepared! The mountain has 25 major glaciers, plus many smaller ones, too. These huge glaciers make the mountain climate extreme.

Up high, you'll experience a world of ice, frost, and bitter cold. But all is not exactly as it seems. If you make it to the **summit**, you may notice steam coming from cracks in the ground. What is going on under Mount Rainier's surface?

Due to its huge size, Mount Rainier often seems as if it's closer than it really is. This field of wildflowers is about six miles (10 km) away from the mountain.

A Big Challenge

Altitude sickness, dangerous weather conditions, or exhaustion keep most climbers from reaching Mount Rainier's summit. The first successful climbers on record were Hazard Stevens and P.B. Van Trump, in 1870. The youngest person ever to reach the summit was a 7-year-old girl!

You might be surprised. Below this steep cone of ice is a **molten** pit of lava. Mount Rainier is actually an active volcano. It could erupt at any time. A volcanic eruption would turn the mountain of ice into a mountain of fire!

You probably don't have much to worry about, however. This sleeping giant has not erupted since the 1840s. Some scientists predict that it won't erupt again for another 500 years. Until then, many people enjoy the challenging climb to its summit. About 10,000 people try it each year. But you must be well-trained. Only about half of these succeed in making it all the way to the top.

People who climb Mount Rainier must be physically fit. It takes a lot of energy to get to the summit! It is also a good idea to have climbed other mountains so that you know what to expect. The journey to the top of Mount Rainier can be dangerous, so climbers must be responsible and careful people.

Longmire and Paradise

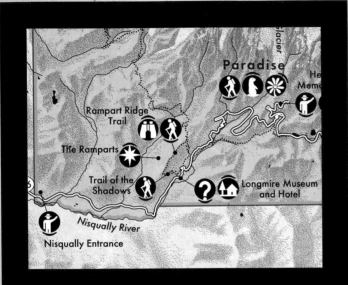

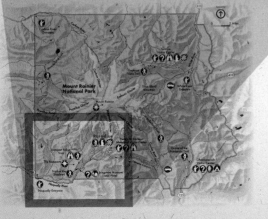

You can enter the park from four sides. The Nisqually entrance, in the southwest corner, is a good place to begin. This entrance is open all year long. You will want to go to Longmire, the park's oldest settlement. Getting there will take you on one of the most beautiful forestland drives in the world. Along the way, look for trees that have been gnawed. This will tell you a beaver has been there.

This area is named for James Longmire, a farmer. Longmire began leading mountain climbing treks here in the 1850s. In 1885, Longmire built Mount Rainier's first hotel.

Take the Trail of the Shadows for an easy, level walk. If you want to work a little harder, though, go for Rampart Ridge Trail. This hike takes you up a steep path. From here, you will get a beautiful view of Mount Rainier. The Ramparts were built up by ancient lava flows. Rainier reached its size through thousands of these flows over the centuries. Each one spilled down from the summit to harden on top of the others.

The Longmire Cabin is along the Trail of the Shadows. James Longmire discovered hot springs in this area in 1883 and built the park's first hotel—Longmire Springs Hotel—in 1890.

Icy Speed Demon

Mount Rainier is the home of America's speediest glacier! During the summer, the Nisqually Glacier moves downhill at a rate of about 16 inches (41 cm) per day. The famed glacier made a record-breaking move in May 1970. That month, it traveled 29 inches (74 cm) inches in a single day!

The Ramparts is also a great place to check out gigantic glaciers. Mount Rainier has more glaciers than any other mountain in the continental United States. These massive chunks of ice can slide downhill as much as 12 inches (30 cm) a day. When they move, they scrape the earth beneath them. This carries rocks and soil down, too. It grinds the ground to bits. This slowly changes the mountain's shape and size.

Paradise is the name of one of the most popular places in the park. The meadows here draw crowds from around the world. In the spring and summer months, these meadows are full of color. Here you'll find rare Indian paintbrush, daisies, buttercups, and pure white avalanche lilies. Lupines add splashes of pink, purple, and yellow. If you stop at a Paradise picnic area, look for red foxes. They show up here often.

In winter, snowfalls are as plentiful as the flowers are in the summer. Paradise averages 680 inches (1,727 cm) of snow a year. That's more than 56 feet (17 m)! In the winter of 1971-72, the area got a total of 93.5 feet (28.5 m). At the time, it was the world record for annual snowfall.

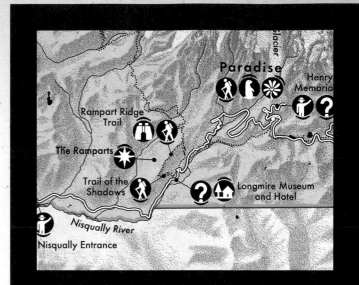

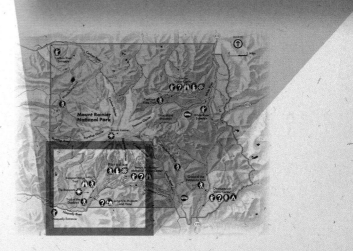

Ancient Trees, Giant Glaciers

A visit to the Ohanapecosh region is a must! This region is located in the park's southeast corner. It combines steep, glacier-carved canyon walls and waterfalls. It is also home to forest areas. Some of nature's most amazing living treasures—and some of its oldest—reside here. To see them for yourself, don't miss the Grove of the **Patriarchs**.

To get there, you will cross a bridge to a misty island. Don't be surprised if you feel very small here. The grove is full of very tall cedar, spruce, fir, and hemlock trees. The trunks of the enormous western red cedars grow to be 25 feet (7.6 m) around. Some Douglas firs have lived more than 1,000 years.

Sunrise is the highest point in the park you can reach by the park roads. The wildflower meadows are beautiful here. This is also one of the best places to see glaciers at close range. Take an easy hike to the Emmons Vista. You will come very near to Emmons glacier. In fact, you'll be right under its enormous overhang. As you gaze upward, you will see just how large this glacier really is! Emmons Glacier is the largest glacier by area in the continental United States.

As you move along the trail, keep your eyes peeled. You might spot some interesting wildlife taking on the heights. These rocky cliffs are home to herds of mountain goats.

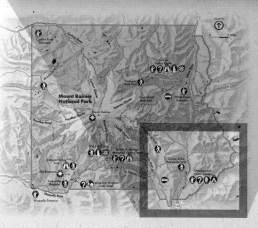

The Grove of the Patriarchs is on an island in the middle of the Ohanapecosh River. Here the trees are protected from fires and floods, which is why they live so long.

Far From the Beaten Track

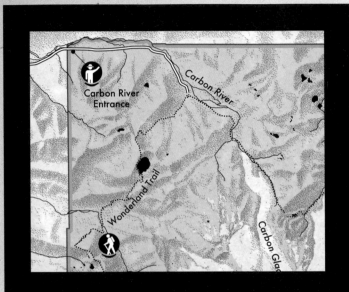

It's time to escape the crowds. The remote Carbon River area is located in the park's northwest corner. You'll find fewer people here because Carbon River is more difficult to reach. The only road into it is through the northwest entrance.

The region is named for the rich underground coal deposits that were once mined here. Now it is a place of nature that is left alone. The Carbon River winds through a damp, foggy world. In some places, the ground seems squishy. You might even feel like you're sinking. You have entered a rare **temperate** rainforest. This is the only true rainforest in the park. It is also one of the last remaining low-level forests of its kind.

🚶🚶 The Carbon River area gets the park's highest rainfall amounts—about 100 inches (254 cm) per year. The river sometimes overflows and floods the one road into the area.

The Sitka spruce, western hemlock, and other varieties of trees form a massive canopy above you. Thick green mosses, ferns, and shrubs make up the forest's dense **understory**.

Keep an eye out for wildlife, too. At dusk, shy black-tailed deer may come out. They like to graze in quiet meadows. If you are lucky, you might see a northern spotted owl. The old-growth forest is home to these rare birds. Park rangers are doing all they can to protect the owls, because they are in danger of becoming extinct.

Muddy Waters

Mount Rainier is the source of five major river systems—the White, Carbon, Puyallup, Nisqually, and Cowlitz. None of these rivers have clear waters. It's not a pollution problem. They are all thick with mud made of finely ground rock that the glaciers have scraped away.

🚶🚶 Here you can see a hemlock tree growing near one of the park's waterfalls. The mist from the falls helps nearby plants and mosses grow thick and green.

25

A World of Wonders

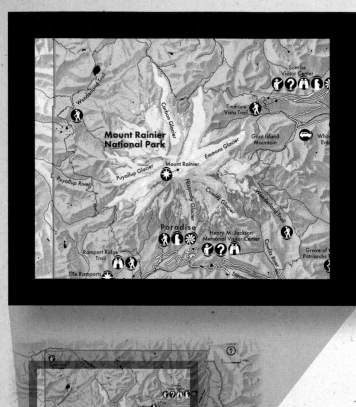

Mount Rainier has shown you many of its wild treasures. If you choose to revisit any of these natural wonders, you can hike the Wonderland Trail. Its 90-mile (145-km) loop is the only way to get all the way around the park without doubling back. Most people allow ten days to two weeks to make the trek. It is one of the best ways to experience Mount Rainier.

No matter how long you visit, nature will cast its spell on you. Wake up as the sun rises over Sunrise. That is when packs of coyotes may be howling. Later, perk up your ears for the high-pitched whistle of a marmot. Sit at sunset beside a roaring Carbon River waterfall. You may hear the distant rumble of falling boulders. These are the voices of Mount Rainier.

🚶🚶 Visitors who travel the Wonderland Trail enjoy some of the most beautiful sites in the park. The trail was opened to visitors in the early 1900s and was later used by rangers to patrol the park. Many of the original ranger cabins are still in use—the oldest of which was built in 1915.

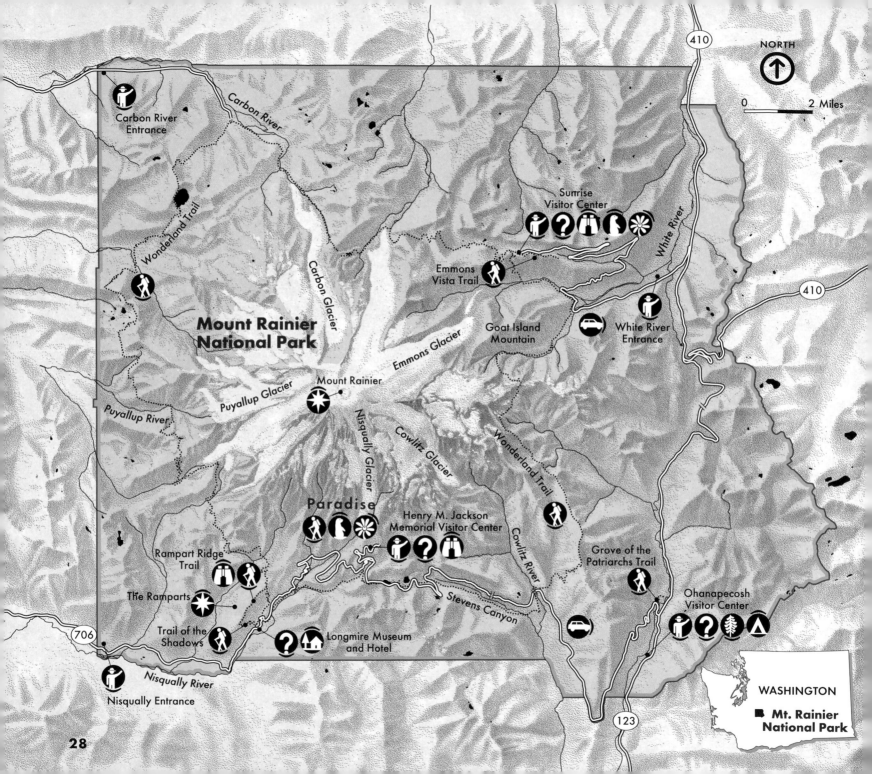

410

NORTH

0   2 Miles

Carbon River
Entrance

Carbon River

Wonderland Trail

Carbon Glacier

**Mount Rainier
National Park**

Sunrise
Visitor Center

White River

Emmons
Vista Trail

410

Emmons Glacier

Goat Island
Mountain

White River
Entrance

Mount Rainier

Puyallup Glacier

Puyallup River

Nisqually Glacier

Cowlitz Glacier

Wonderland Trail

Paradise

Henry M. Jackson
Memorial Visitor Center

Cowlitz River

Grove of the
Patriarchs Trail

Rampart Ridge
Trail

Ohanapecosh
Visitor Center

The Ramparts

Stevens Canyon

Trail of the
Shadows

Longmire Museum
and Hotel

706

Nisqually River

Nisqually Entrance

123

WASHINGTON

■ **Mt. Rainier
National Park**

MOUNT RAINIER NATIONAL PARK FAST FACTS

Date founded: March 2, 1899

Location: Central Washington

Size: 365 square miles/945 sq km; 233,600 acres/ 94,535 hectares

Major habitats: Temperate rainforest, old-growth forest, tundra, subalpine meadows, and alpine glaciers

Important landforms: Mount Rainier, Nisqually Glacier, Carbon Glacier, Emmons Glacier, Cowlitz-Ingraham Glacier, and the Ramparts

Elevation:
   Highest: 14,410 feet/4,392 m (Columbia Crest)
   Lowest: 1,610 feet/490.7 m

Weather:
   Average yearly rainfall: 75 inches/190.5 cm (Ohanapecosh); 87 inches/221 cm (Longmire); 126 inches/320 cm (Paradise)
   Average yearly snowfall: 635 inches/1,613 cm (Paradise)
   Hottest temperature: 81 F/27 C (Ohanapecosh)
   Coolest temperature: –18 F/–28 C (Paradise)

Number of animal species: 54 species of mammals, 126 kinds of birds, 17 amphibian and reptiles species, and 8 species of fish

Main animal species: Chipmunks, black-tailed deer, coyotes, red foxes, Douglas' squirrels, golden-mantled ground squirrels, gray jays, Steller's jays, Clark's nutcrackers, and ravens

Number of plant species: 787

Main plant species: Douglas fir and western hemlock make up most of the old-growth forest

Number of endangered or threatened animal species: 6—marbled murrelet, northern spotted owl, peregrine falcon, bald eagle, Chinook salmon, and bull trout

Native people: Nisqually, Puyallup, Upper Cowlitz, Yakama, and Muckleshoot

Number of visitors each year: About 2 million

Important sites and landmarks: National Park Inn, Wonderland Trail, Goat Island Mountain, Stevens Canyon, Grove of the Patriarchs, and Nisqually River suspension bridge

Tourist activities: Hiking, boating, canoeing, fishing, horseback riding, mountain climbing, wildlife viewing, snowshoeing, cross-country skiing, snowmobiling, and snowboarding

GLOSSARY

conservation (kon-ser-VAY-shun): Conservation is the careful and planned protection of something, especially a natural resource. Most people agree that the conservation of America's wilderness areas is important for plants, animals, and people.

diverse (dy-VURSS): Things that are distinctly different from one another are said to be diverse. Mount Rainier's alpine meadows contain an extremely diverse group of wildflowers.

ecosystem (EE-koh-sis-tum): Plants and animals that live together and depend on one another for life create an ecosystem. The rainforest ecosystem could easily be destroyed if logging were permitted.

glacier (GLAY-shur): A glacier is a huge slab of ice that spreads across the land or moves slowly down a slope. The Nisqually Glacier moves faster than most.

molten (MOLT-un): A molten substance is one that has been turned into liquid by intense heat. The extreme heat within the earth melts rocks into molten liquid.

patriarchs (PAY-tree-arks): The oldest fathers of a group of people are often known as the patriarchs. Mount Rainier's oldest trees are called patriarchs because they are like ancient fathers to the rest of the forest.

species (SPEE-sheez): A species is a group of living things that shares physical traits distinguishing them from other living things. The rattlesnake is a different species of snake than the cobra.

summit (SUM-mit): The highest level, or peak, of a mountain is called its summit. It takes about two days to climb to the summit of Mount Rainier.

temperate (TEM-puh-rut): When something is temperate (such as weather), it is neither very hot nor very cold. A temperate rainforest can be found in the Carbon River area.

understory (UN-der-stor-ee): The layer of trees and plants that grows between the forest floor and the highest treetops is called the understory. The understory in many forests is thick with shrubs, bushes, and small trees.

TO FIND OUT MORE

Λ

FURTHER READING

Brimner, Larry Dane.
Glaciers.
New York: Children's Press, 2000.

Luenn, Nancy and Pierr Morgan (illustrator).
Miser on the Mountain: A Nisqually Legend of Mount Rainier.
Seattle, WA: Sasquatch Books, 1997.

Nelson, Sharlene and Ted Nelson.
Mount Rainier National Park.
New York: Children's Press, 1998.

ON THE WEB

Visit our home page for lots of links about
Mount Rainier National Park:

http://www.childsworld.com/links

NOTE TO PARENTS, TEACHERS, AND LIBRARIANS:
We routinely check our Web links to make sure
they're safe, active sites—so encourage your
readers to check them out!

INDEX

Carbon River, 22, *23*, 26

early visitors, *9*
ecosystem, 9
elk, 6, 7
Emmons Glacier, 20

glaciers, 6, 12, 18, 19, 20, 24
Grove of the Patriarchs, 20, *21*

hemlock tree, 20, 24, *25*
hotel, 16, *17*

lava, 14, 16
Longmire, 16
Longmire Cabin, *17*
Longmire, James, 16, *17*

marmots, 8, 26
meadows, 6, 19, 20
mountain climbers, 14, *15*
mountain goats, 20
Mount Rainier, *11*, 12, *13*, 14, *15*, 16, 18, 19, 24

Nisqually Glacier, 18
northern spotted owl, 24

Ohanapecosh region, 20
old-growth forest, 24

Pacific Ocean, 10
Paradise, 19

rain, 10, *11*, 19, *23*

rainforest, 6, 22
Ramparts, The, 16, 19
river systems, 24

snow, 10, *11*, 19
summer, 10, 18, 19
Sunrise, 20, 26

Trail of the Shadows, 16, *17*
trees, 6, 16, 20, *21*, 24

volcano, 14

wildflowers, 6, 8, *13*, 19, 20
winter, 10, 19
Wonderland Trail, 26, *27*